Mankind may never

make it!

Osborn

MANKIND MAY NEVER MAKE IT!

BY ROBERT *Chesley* OSBORN

NEW YORK GRAPHIC SOCIETY

GREENWICH · CONNECTICUT

Library of Congress Catalogue Card No. 68-16742. Printed in Weert, Holland by Smeets Lithographers.

Published by NEW YORK GRAPHIC SOCIETY LTD., Greenwich, Connecticut. Acknowledgments of photographs: page 1 by Ruth Block; Robert Osborn by Elodie Courter; page 39 courtesy of Mainichi Shimbun, Tokyo, Japan; page 51 courtesy of Culberson.

NTRODUCTION

This book is about man's nature and behavior and
what can come of it.

I have long since tired of all the feathery words and
vague hopes of what man *must* do or *ought* to do.

I have tried to assemble what he *does*, and *can* do.

R.O.

Mankind *thinks* he'll make it through

regardless of what he does . . . .

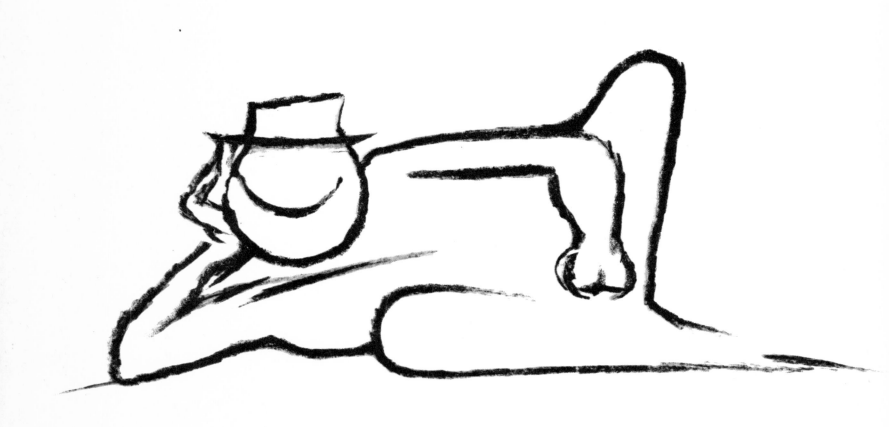

or does *not* do.

He happily *assumes* that
he will survive.

Of course he won't, if he doesn't recognize
the trend of events and the forces at work.

The hard facts gainsay his hopeful vagaries. His life grows more complex; his dangers proliferate . . . and worst of all the nature of his psyche too often inhibits his decisions and actions.

The *next* years will cast his predicament in iron . . . . to the point of final disaster . . . . if he does not resist . . . . does not preserve his freedom of choice . . . . . and *use* it.

MAN'S GREATEST FAILURE IS HIS *UNWILLINGNESS*

TO MAKE EACH *CRITICAL* CHOICE

to make decisions and make them *clearly* . . .

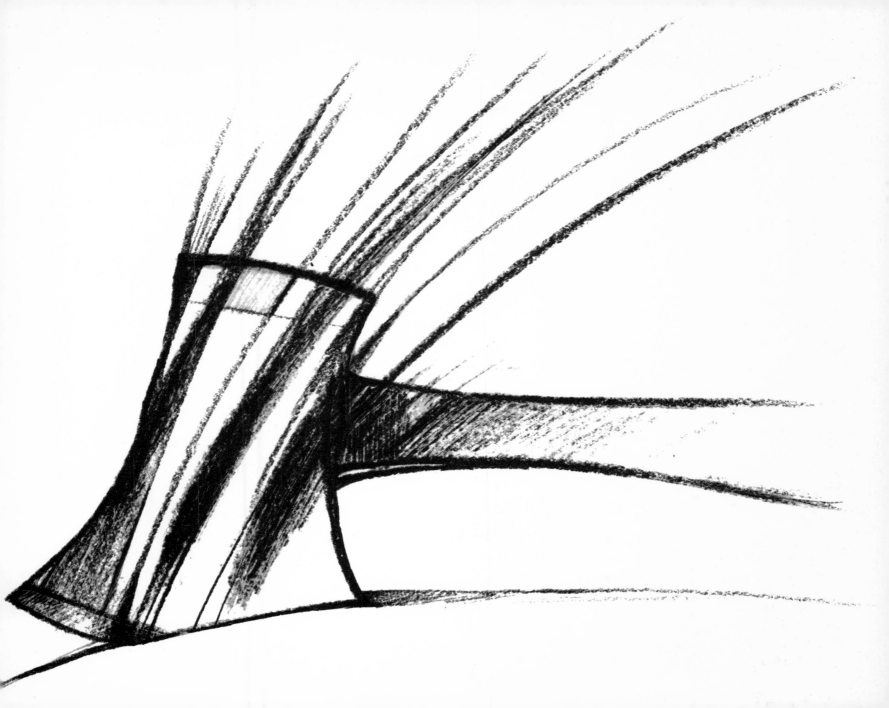

and to make them in sufficient numbers and then to ACT on them.

In a world of inexorable change and effect . . . . each failure

compounds each previous failure.

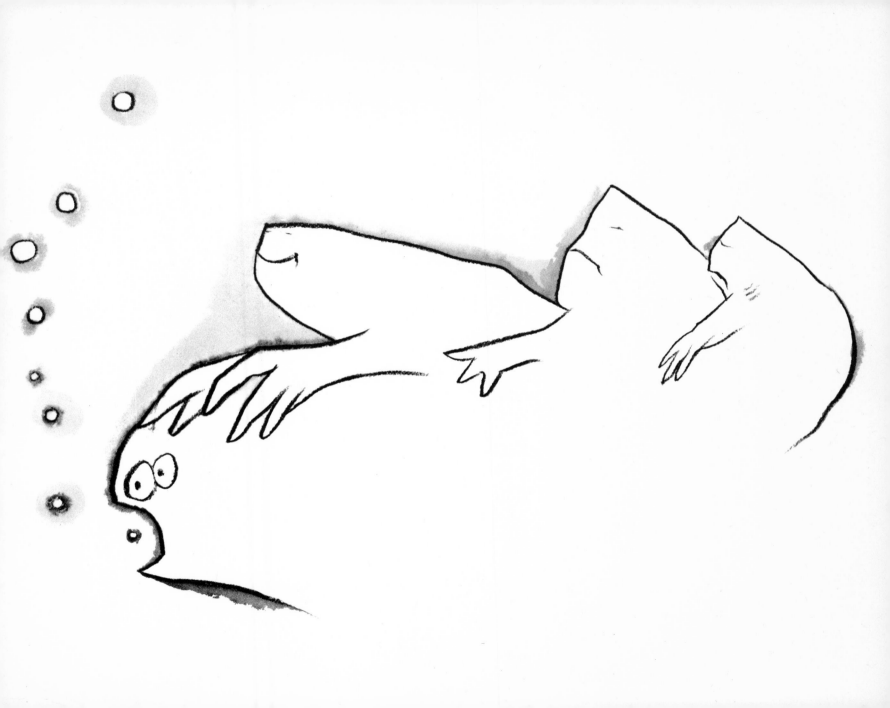

Man is carelessly destroying his environment; he befouls

his nest to the point of death.

He swallows the once beautiful land and regurgitates it in a *chaos* called URBAN SPRAWL and does this relentlessly and without shame,

for the ACQUISITIVE INSTINCT is strong and cunning.

Mechanization and cybernetics have so dehumanized man's environment and so dislocated and repressed his simplest body needs that his psyche erupts and aborts in all manner of violence . . . . vandalism . . . . and mental illness.

Yet adults continue to sell themselves on the mechanized environment

. . . . and its endless detritus . . . . as a way of life.

Though man is fecund as a fruit fly he can not surmount his

antique religious beliefs, his unctuous mores . . . . and act to

CONTROL his reproduction.

India is trying to.

In one year the government interested 800,000 (thousand) potent

women and some men in birth control . . . . but in the same year

its population of 485,000,000 (million) was INCREASING at

the rate of ONE MILLION EVERY *MONTH* . . . .

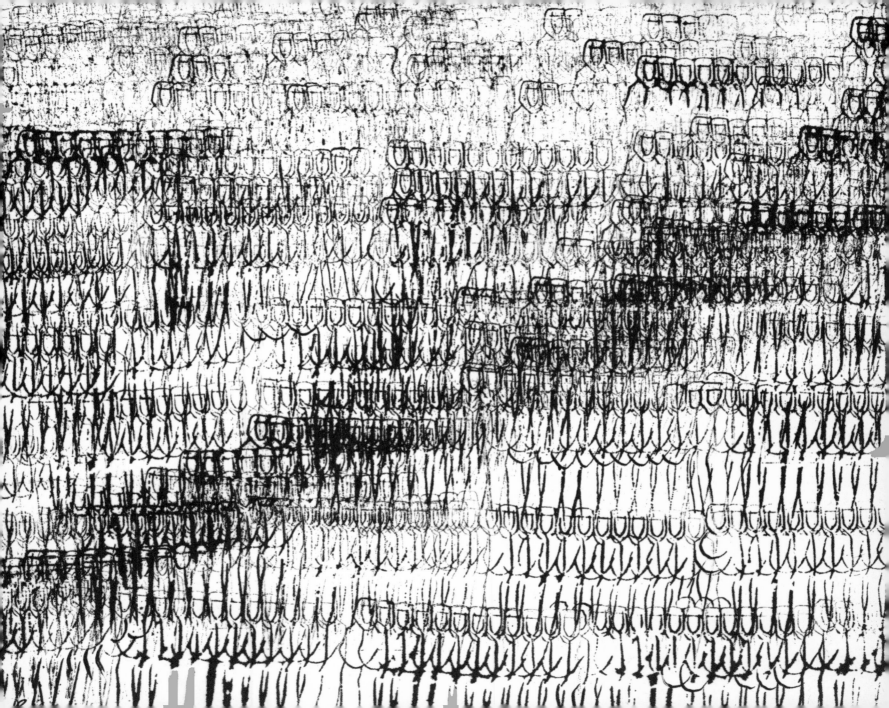

and this in a land where grinding poverty and hunger already exist . . . . .

and *education* for the new-born does *not!*

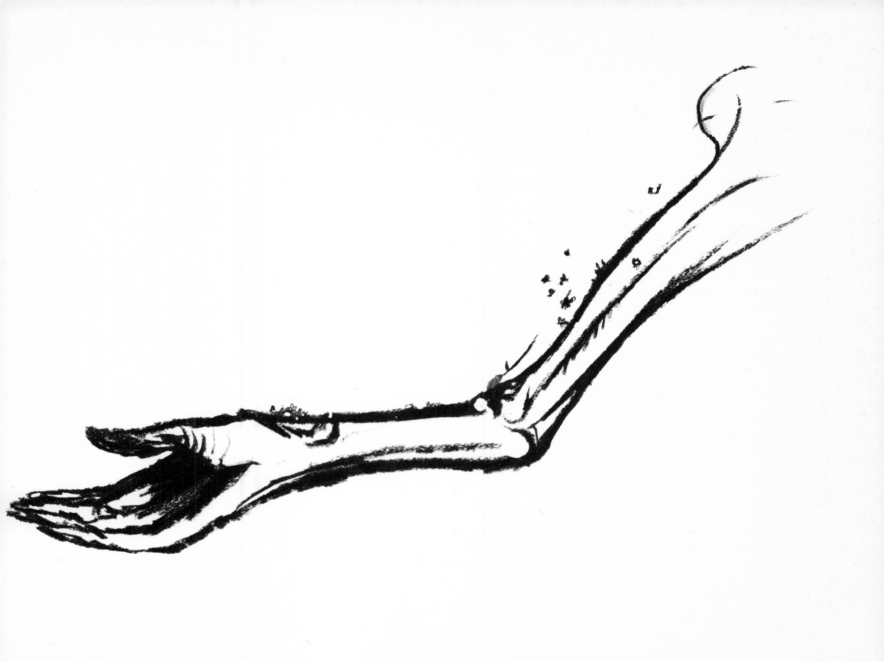

Man is presently reproducing himself at such a rate that more people will be born on the earth in the next forty years than have been born on the earth since Cro-Magnon man.

Confronted by such a fact, one would expect clear and determined

action to stem the tide . . . . .

for we KNOW that TWO out of every three human beings alive this

day will lie down tonight hungry, or cold, or BOTH.

At this point don't give up hope and slit *your* throat!

For we also KNOW that MAN, unlike all other living forms has a mind

of incredible capacity and discreteness. He can perceive the present . . . .

and also *himself* . . . . recall the past . . . . and *imagine* the future!

THIS capacity may in the end save us!

Too, *half* of our being LOVES and is life-giving . . . . . can *create* all manner of things . . . . is BIO-PHILIC. This too may save us!

This loving part can exhibit an unbelievable unselfishness in its capacity for kindness, understanding, and sacrifice for other human beings. It comprehends and is excited by the *relation* between all men and women. It disdains insular tribes. It longs to love and be loved. It invites and creates *life*.

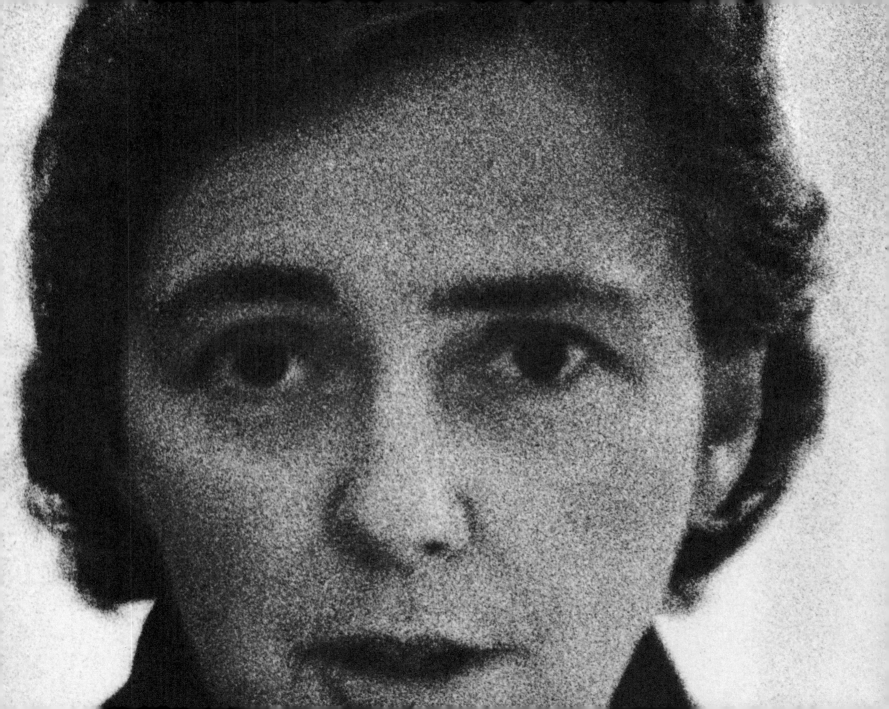

Unfortunately there is the other side of it. Half of our psyche

HATES, ... is HOSTILE, *fearful,* and NECRO-PHILIC.

Whether we like it or not, whether we admit it or not . . . .

it is THIS half of us which deals in all manner of death, both

monstrous and subtle.

In my life the Military has killed 64 *MILLION* of its own species.

NO OTHER LIFE FORM SO VICIOUSLY DESTROYS

ITSELF . . . . ONLY *MAN*.

And because he can not inhibit his aggressiveness, he

ritualizes it to make such carnage PALATABLE!

He massively *STARVED* two million in the plains and passes

because it suited *his* small purposes.

He has burned them in ovens . . . glistening black . . .

six million of them.

Yet out of the memory of his barbarity he STILL does not

organize a lawful ORDER between ALL human beings.

Instead he cautiously establishes a

League of Nations or United Nations but carefully

writes in the vitiating VETO power.

He did not bring China into the community of nations when he could have . . . . . although a quarter of the people on this earth are Chinese.

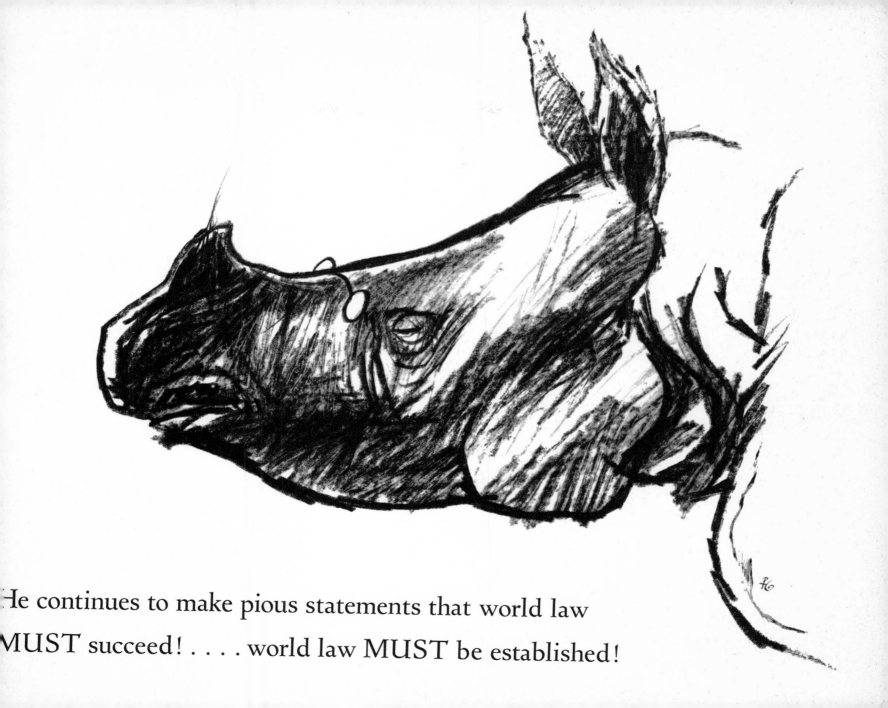

He continues to make pious statements that world law
MUST succeed! . . . . world law MUST be established!

But national purposes remain starkly national, insular, and *self*-protective . . .

. . . openly aggressive and full of HATE!

Statesmen brazenly use FORCE whenever and wherever they wish.

THEY MUMBLE IN THEIR HELMETS. They are not devoted to the cause of Peace.

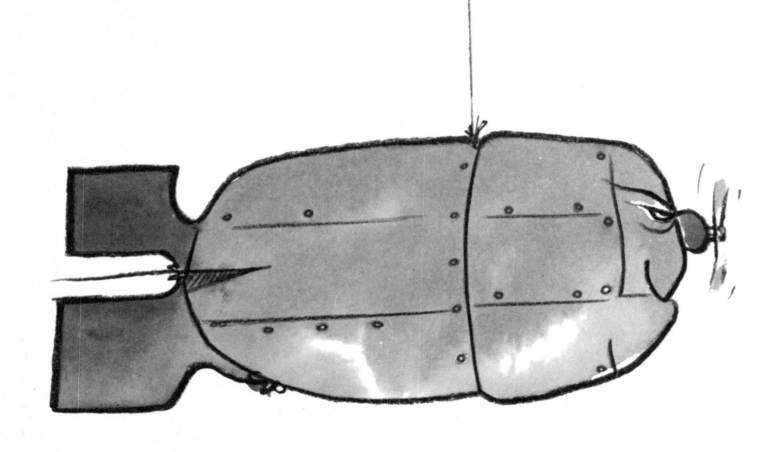

ON JUNE 24, 1944 THE BOMB WAS EXPLODED HERE

It was called "FAT BOY."

Until that moment mankind was able to survive and to recover from the losses Nature or his own craven brutality inflicted upon him.

That era is ended.

Isolated nations can now cast a lingering scarf

of death around the world to kill even those

at peace with themselves in small and distant lands.

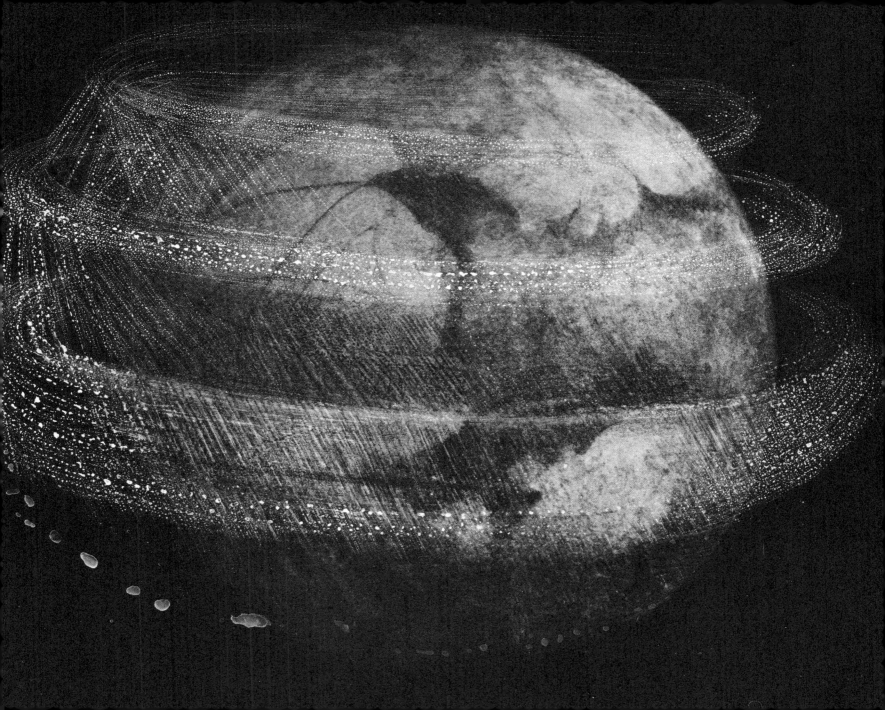

For strontium loves us all.

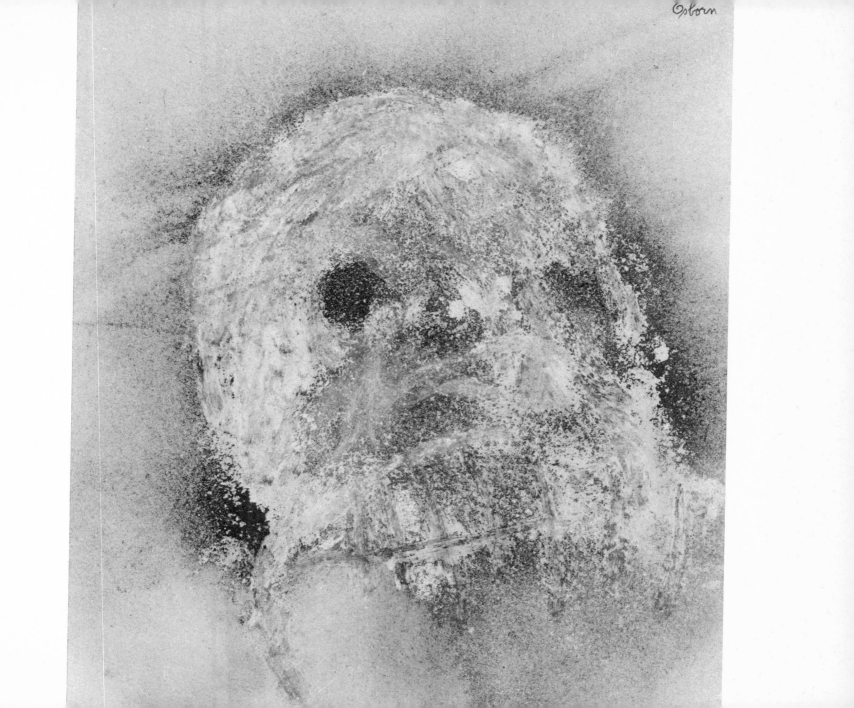

And the sobering fact is:
  no matter what we pretend,
    no matter what we say,

man has never produced a
major invention and left it unused.

He always says he won't but he does!

Even stopping the *proliferation* of the bombs is proving painful and

difficult. They spread now like mushrooms . . . . and in one nuclear power

after another the Military (like rodents) dig their rockets deep into the

earth and carefully point them at their fellow man.

It is not the young who do this, it is the old.

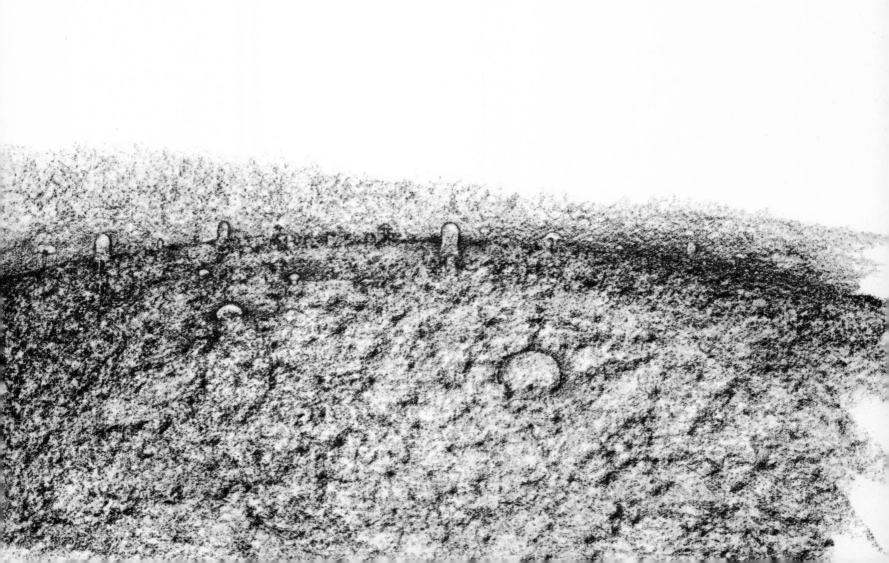

Or they can now load *ONE* bomber with more explosive force than was

unleashed in *ALL* of World War II.

And most destructive of all, their anesthetized Military minds add

bacteria and gases to their arsenal . . . . just to be *sure*.

They have isolated a botulin so virulent

that slightly more than a pound . . . 500 grams . . .

can wipe out the world's population.

Technology is now

sufficiently advanced

o destroy itself

in a matter of days.

However, against this drift towards death there is a new force at work. The almost intuitive and rising sense that all men are related rather than enemies . . . . are more similar than dissimilar . . . . that they *can* work together.

And here's a truly hopeful sign: among the young in many different lands and races there is this new approach. At last the young are pursuing the *unity* of man, no longer his fragmentation.

For the alternative is DEADLY.

But because man can foresee it,

he can avoid it.

It will not just happen.

It requires WORK, and resistance, and creation

to attain it, but it *can* be attained.

Eric Fromm has said it well: "Man's heart can harden; it can become inhuman, yet never nonhuman. It always remains man's heart. We all are determined by the fact that we have been born human, and hence by the never-ending task of having to make choices. We must choose the means together with the aims. We must not rely on anyone's saving us, but be very aware of the fact that wrong choices make us incapable of saving ourselves."